# THE ROLE OF UNJHA MARKET YARD

# IN MARKETING OF AGRICULTURAL

# PRODUCTS

:: Author ::

## Dr. Chirag V. Raval

(M.COM., M.Phil., Ph.D.)

## PUBLISHED BY

**The New ERa International Publishing House**
**HQ. At & Po. Chaveli., Ta- Chansma,**
**Dist- Patan, North Gujarat, India, Asia.**
www.iphouseindia.com

First Publication: 18th January, 2015

**ISBN:- 978-15-08675-68-6**

Price: Rs.750/- INDIA

$ 15 OUTSIDE INDIA

**PUBLISHED BY**

**The New ERa International Publishing House**
HQ. At & Po. Chaveli., Ta- Chansma,
Dist- Patan, North Gujarat, India, Asia.
www.iphouseindia.com

# <u>Index</u>

| Sr. No. | Contents | Page No. |
|---------|----------|----------|
|  | Acknowledgement |  |
| 1. | Introduction | 01 |
| 2. | Growth of Agriculture | 32 |
| 3. | About Unjha Market Yard | 52 |
| 4. | Research Methodology | 59 |
| 5. | Results | 64 |
| 6. | Findings and Suggestions | 70 |
|  | References | 74 |

## ACKNOWLEDGEMENT

I am deeply indebted and wish to express my sincere gratitude to my "Guruji" Dr. R.M.Joshi (Reader),P.G.Dept. of Business Studies, Sardar Patel University, Vallabh Vidhyanagar. for his invaluable guidance, encouragement, critical comments and constant inspiration throughout the course of this investigation.

A word of thank cannot suffice the great efforts taken by my teacher Shri. R.M. Rathod and Faculties, P.G. Development of business Studies, Sardar Patel University, Vallabh Vidhyanagar.

The word fails me to express my greatest inspiration, constant encouragement, blessing, moral and emotional support as well as love of my family members Mr. Rajendra V. Raval, Mrs. Sweta R.Raval, Mr. Kalpesh V.Raval, Mrs. Poonam K.Raval and lovable nephew Shivani and Pransy.

Lastly but not least, I thank all who directly and

indirectly helped me in successful completion of this work.

Finally thanks do not seen enough to the almighty to whom I owe everything.

**(Chirag V. Raval)**

# Chapter 1
## Introduction

Agriculture in India has always been India's most important economics sector. India's 70 percentage population depends upon agriculture sector. Agricultural is base of Indian mossolium of India endeavors on industries. The speedy development of the Indian economy may be made possible only with the development of agriculture. India is also well known as "The Home of Spices". India share in world market of spices has been increased a lot on account of the advantages EXIM policy of the government. Agriculture, agricultural research agricultural development even in minute term are as important for India as Electronic for Japan, Flower farming for Israel, and Automation and Automobile for the U.S.A. It is a high time for India to achieve mastery and prompt development in this agricultural field.

The word agriculture means production of crops of various types. The agricultural allied activities encompass horticulture, Sericulture .plantation, diary and dairy products, livestock, fishing and the rearing of pigs. Both agricultural and its allied activities are in combination and not separable in rural life. Hence in general the Term 'Agriculture' connotes all the above activities. The villager is growing more cash crops and not traditional cereal production. The modern ideas like irrigation, time cycle, and productivity per acre are sweeping the villages. Job mobility is on the increase. The main rural occupation is still agriculture and will continue to be so as agriculture provides basic food grains to the masses.

## Concept

As a concept, how and when agriculture originated is an interesting question. Man started as a hunter, then progressed to food gathering and thereafter become a cultivator. It has been slow evolutionary process. Man learnt the art of agriculture and developed it into a systemic science with his constant observation, trials and efforts. Agricultural is as old as modern man for many centuries. It has and even today is the main stay of livelihood of man. This is particularly true of underdeveloped countries.

Social thinkers Alvin and Heidi Toffler in their book "Creating a New Civilization" have divided human technological economy in three waves as under:

| I Wave - Agriculture | 8000 BC to 1750 AD (Peak 1650 AD to 1750 AD) | Agriculture |
| II Wave – Industry | 1750 AD to 1840 AD | Steam Power |
| | 1840 AD to 1890 AD | Rail |
| | 1890 AD to 1980 AD | Electrical Power |
| III Wave – IT & | 1980 AD to 2030 AD | Bioengineering including Genetic |
| High Technology | 2030 AD to 2080 AD | Engineering and Nano Engineering |

Since the last four decades, there is perceptible changes in economies. The industry sector and the service sectors have been contributing more and surging in economic development Nevertheless, the importance of agriculture remains, in view of the fact that for about half the global population, agriculture and allied activities are main occupations. An eminent economist Dr. Gunnar said "It is in the agricultural sector that the battle for the long term economic development will be won or lost".

In the Asian context, development means rural development, since most Asian communities live In villages. India 1ives in its villages where Agriculture is the main occupation Hence agriculture has become the backbone of the Indian economy.

## Definition of Agricultural Marketing

A simple definition of agricultural marketing is buying and selling of agricultural produce. In the olden days, when villages were self sufficient and self contained, the fanners used to barter or sell their produce in the village market. The above simple definition suits this type of village market. Today the agricultural markets have evolved. There are stages and interdependence in the agricultural marketing activities. The agricultural produce changes many hands before it reaches the end user.

Second definition is 'agricultural market is a place where agricultural produce is brought and sold.' This definition is narrow and importance is given to place only.

The third definition as per Indian Council of Agricultural Research is "Agricultural Marketing involves three important functions:

(i) Assembling or concentration of goods

(ii) Preparation for consumption and

(iii) Distribution of agricultural products."

The fourth definition as per American Association is: "Marketing includes all activities having to do with affecting changes in ownership and possession of goods and services. It is that part of economics which deals with creation of time, place, and possession utilities and that phase of business activity through which human wants are satisfied by exchange of goods and services for some valuable considerations."

The fifth definition as per National Commission on Agricultural (NCA) is: "Agricultural Marketing is a process which starts with a decision to produce a saleable farm commodity, and it involves all aspects of marketing structure or system, both functional and institutional, based o technical and economic considerations and include pre-harvest and post-harvest operations of

(i) Assembling,

(ii) Grading,

(iii) Storage,

(iv) Transportation and

(v) Distribution".

The NCA definition gives an overall view of agricultural marketing and gives an overall view of agricultural marketing due importance to promoting economic development. Marketing has become a tool and multiplier of economic development. If there are no good and reasonable returns, no farmer will be interested in increasing.

**INDIAN AGRICULTURE :** The per capita availability of a number of food items in India increased significantly in the post-independence period despite a population increase from 361 million in 1951 to 846 million in 1991. Per capita availability of cereals went up from 334 grams per day in 1951 to 470 grams per day in

1990. Availability of edible oils increased significantly, from 3.2 kilograms per year per capita in FY 1960 to 5.4 kilograms in FY 1990. Similarly, the availability of sugar per capita increased from 4.7 to 12.5 kilograms per year during the same period. The one area in which availability decreased was pulses, which went from 60.7 grams per day to 39.4 grams per day. This shortfall presents a serious problem in a country where a large part of the population is vegetarian and pulses are the main source of protein.

There are large disparities among India's states and territories in agricultural performance, only some of which can be attributed to differences in climate or initial endowments of infrastructure such as irrigation. Realizing the importance of Indian agricultural production for economic development, the central government has played an active role in all aspects of agricultural development. Planning is centralized, and plan priorities, policies, and resource allocations are decided at the central level. Food and price policy also are decided by the central government. Thus, although agriculture in India is constitutionally the responsibility of the states rather than the central government, the latter plays a key role in formulating policy and providing financial resources for agriculture.

The agriculture sector is important for food security, employment generation and economic growth. However, concern has now been expressed on the decline in agricultural growth. Modern agriculture is knowledge-based, in which education at all levels, particularly higher education has an important role.

Agriculture in India has always been INDIA'S most important economic sector. In the mid-1990s, it provides approximately one-third of the gross domestic product and employs roughly two-thirds of the population. Since independence in 1947, the share of agriculture in India in the GDP has declined in comparison to the growth of the industrial and services sectors. However, agriculture in India still provides the bulk of wage goods required by the nonagricultural sector as well as numerous raw materials for industry. Moreover, the direct share of agricultural and allied sectors in total exports is around 18 percent. When the indirect share of agricultural products in total exports, such as cotton textiles and jute goods, is taken into account, the percentage is much higher. Expansion in crop production, therefore, has to come almost entirely from increasing yields on lands already in some kind of agricultural use.

The project covers 225 APMC yards and taluka headquarters in Gujarat, but it is only a pilot project that the Forward Markets Commission (FMC) plans to take up at the national level in the coming years. The NMCE has already installed about 50 such boards in different APMCs and taluka headquarters of Gujarat and is now making an effort to encourage farmers to use the information flowing on the boards.

At Unjha, the world's largest market for psyllum husk (Isabgol) and cumin seed, farmers say that the ticker board could have been useful had it been put at a better place. "The ticker board has been put at `Rain Basera', which is a waiting room where nobody goes to see it. It should be put up in a more prominent place so that more people can see it. With the onset of the season, farmers will come from all over, they should get to see it and benefit from the information," says Praveen Patel, a leading cumin seed trader at Unjha.

"The benefits of the ticker boards are manifold. Farmers can see what commodities are quoting at an attractive price in the futures and take an informed decision on what to sow. Traders can also benefit by the whole process of transparent price discovery that the commodity exchanges enable,".

1. An efficient marketing system is one of the pre-requisites for raising the income of the farmers. The available marketing facilities and different marketing channels bring variation in the net price got by the producer-farmers for the produce disposed of by them. The farmers' behavior with

respect to sale of their surplus produce and the pattern of flow of surplus produce in the marketing channels is influenced by number of factors as proximity to market, availability of market, price of the produce in the market, availability of transport facilities, available storage facility, financial position of the farmers, etc.

As, I searched for a special area of market for my search work, the agricultural produce market committee Unjha, in North Gujarat flashed on my mind at first. Because Unjha Market Yard of Gujarat state is the well known international market for sale Cumin, Fennel, Isabgul, etc, in the country, So, I choose the Unjha Market Yard for my research work.

## Objectives of Agricultural Marketing

Agricultural marketing is the engine of growth for the agricultural sector. It can make or break the economic system and its growth. The objectives can be put as:

(i)    Rotation of economic resource

(ii)  Development

(iii)  Increase in productivity of economy

(iv)  Widen product ranges

(v)  Stratezise and plan for success

(vi)  Bring in consumer satisfaction

(vii) Bring good marketing practices and

(viii)   Develop a pool of managerial talent

(i) **Rotation of economic resources**: Marketing makes full use of economic assets and productive capacity available at a point of time. It also mobilises latest economic potential. It has active and constructive role in channelising the resources. It improves economy, its efficiency and effectiveness. Increase in productivity of the economy increases national income. A planned agricultural marketing.

•     Increases scope of economic activities: Investments in agricultural areas generate sales and employment opportunities manifold. This has a multiplier effect and acts as booster. Increased incomes and effects of advertisement generate more spending. This gives more employment and the cycle expands.

• Focusses on proper and timely market research: With scientific market studies, the demand can be forecasted and projects drawn on realistic data. Many projects fail because of nil or poor market study and analysis.

**(ii) Development:** Low marketing activities give rise to underdevelopment. Underdevelopment breeds unemployment and the vicious circle continues. To bring in development, a good and forward looking marketing programme is a must. This is specially true for underdeveloped countries. The reasons are:

• Good marketing increases consumption: The individual is encouraged to consume more and more. It is an important economic multiplier. More consumption and more production give more income and innovation. Thus marketing acts as booster to economic activities

**(iii)Increase in productivity of economy:** Because of increase in demand, the production and productivity increases. Productivity enhances economic activities and growth. This gives rise to upswing chain effect. Marketing becomes a coordinator in:

Mobilising the resources:   The economic resource mobilisation is the first step. Marketing motivates general public to save and invest in agriculture and marketing.

Making the operation profitable increase in production and productivity makes products cost competitive. Profit orientation is the centre point of any marketing activity. More profits bring more capital. The expansion of market activities and exporting of agricultural produce increase.

Bring utility: marketing creates utility: Basically advertising beings in utility. The consumer is educated about new products and models. The consumer perceives a product or a service. Creation of a utility perception in the minds of consumers enhances marketing activities.

**(iv) Widen product range:** Marketing increases the consumer base and enlarge demand in quantities and variety of requirement to meet the needs of group and regions. Products could be manufacture in small scale or large scale as per demands of a particular verity or range. For example, many types' fruits are imported and sold because of demand. The prices of these fruits are high, and there are customers who pay these high prices. If there is a good market, these fruits may be grown in India in the near future.

(v) **Stratezise and plan for success:** Evolving a long range vision or strategy and breaking this into apian of activities is an important activity of good agricultural marketing. Good planning also includes coordinating and integrating the inputs to arrive at the desired output. The resources are geared and augmented to meet the plans. Marketing helps in improving distribution systems and maintaining high levels of production.

**(vi) Bring in consumer satisfaction:** The marketing activities are developed around the consumer and bring in the following factors:

• Consumer Delight: The consumer is satisfied because he gets choice of goods he needs at competitive prices. The products are easily available and near his place.

•      Benefit to consumer: Utilisation of full capacity of production brings in cost economies. Marketing converts seller's market into a buyer's market

•      Improvement in service: After sales service has become a mantra of marketing. The service aspect gives the customer a mental security and feel good factor makes him buy. With the expanding market, the service aspect in marketing is gaining importance.

**(vii)Bring good marketing practices:** The agricultural marketing can bring changes in the mindsets from a ration officers mental set up lo competitive marketing. It's appropriate to make marketing a planned goal oriented effort instead of leaving it to chances.

**(viii)  Match  the  environment  factors:** Proper environment plays a key role in development of agricultural marketing. The factors are broadly grouped:

• Micro environment and

• Macro environment

• Micro environment - includes different constituents of marketing like intermediately agencies, government agencies and consumers. These agencies in turn are part of the macro environment where all arc affected.

• Macro environment factors - these are changing conditions surrounding the marketing activity. These are:

- Government and legal environment

- Economy environment

- Socio-cultural factors

- Technology

- Political factors and

- Climate and natural factors.

(ix) Develop a pool of managerial talent: Good entrepreneurial managers are required to manage challenging jobs of agricultural marketing. There are agricultural resources available whereas result-oriented managers are to be trained. Managers with a positive attitude and capable of taking decisions are required. A training on the job in marketing exposes an entrant in new and challenging areas of consumer behaviour, business problems, competition and innovations. Marketing in agricultural produce can give ground to new emerging or future managerial cadre.

**Scope and Subject Matter**

Agricultural market environment leads the scope of any system. Evolving proper plans and marketing methods for agricultural produce is necessary. The points for improving the scope are:

**(i) Due importance to cooperative institutions:** Co-operative movement is based on the spirit of working together and coming together. The movement which started in India in 1904, is based on basics of "everybody for all and all for everybody". The Co-operative movement, an integral part in Indian rural development in general and agricultural marketing in particular. Co-operative institutions that are existing should be activated and geared for marketing activities.

**(ii) Co-ordination with procurement agencies:** Public procurement agencies are large buyers marketing should co-ordinate and work for better prices and timely procurement actions.

**(iii) Demand side management:** Marketing of agricultural produce calls for good estimation of demand and time schedules. This is a scientific and continuous exercise. The cropping patterns be planned accordingly.

**(iv) Market studies and market intelligence:** Modern communication systems and television help in rural areas to improve market studies. Computers help for close estimation and faster calculations and reports. The market details like daily arrivals, quality, market surpluses average prices and demand for different varieties of data can be collected quickly for better and strategic decision-making.

**(v) Price policy:** Based on computerised data, price to consumers can be decided.

**(vi) Grading facilities:** Grade specifications should be laid well to arrive at uniform quality. The specification also should be adhered to and given wide publicity.

**(vii) Storage facilities:** Credits also should be linked to stocks properly stored in modern storage facilities.

Modern and cold storage facilities at a cluster of villages help agricultural produce marketing.

**(viii)** Finance arrangement and planning goes a long way in marketing effective and

**(x)Education to farmers:** Farmers should be educate in modern technique of production, quality and marketing methods.

Apart from the above nine areas of improvement, agricultural marketing has to be actively involved in all stages of marketing to generate demand activate intermediate producer to reach the final consumer. These functions are

(i) Follow-up and assembling the farm produce

(ii) Proper grading of the farm produce

(iii) Handling, packing and shifting

(iv) Proper storage of the agricultural produce

(v) Processing of the agricultural produce

(vi) Making ready the products for marketing

(vii) Handling and transportation to marketing centres

(viii) Arranging finances for the entire cycle

(ix) Risk bearing of the produce and

(x) Distribution of the agricultural produce to the final coustmer.

**Challenges in Agricultural Marketing**

The agricultural market is growing at a faster pace since the last four decades and adjusting itself to new socio-economic conditions. Important changes that have happened are:

- **Green Revolution;** Agricultural productivity has increased due to different measures taken:
- Improved seed quality
- Emphasis by successive five year plans of the Government of India giving thrust to the agricultural sector.

The comparative structure of the tenth plan and ninth plan are given below:

*Comparison of 9th and 10th five year Plans*

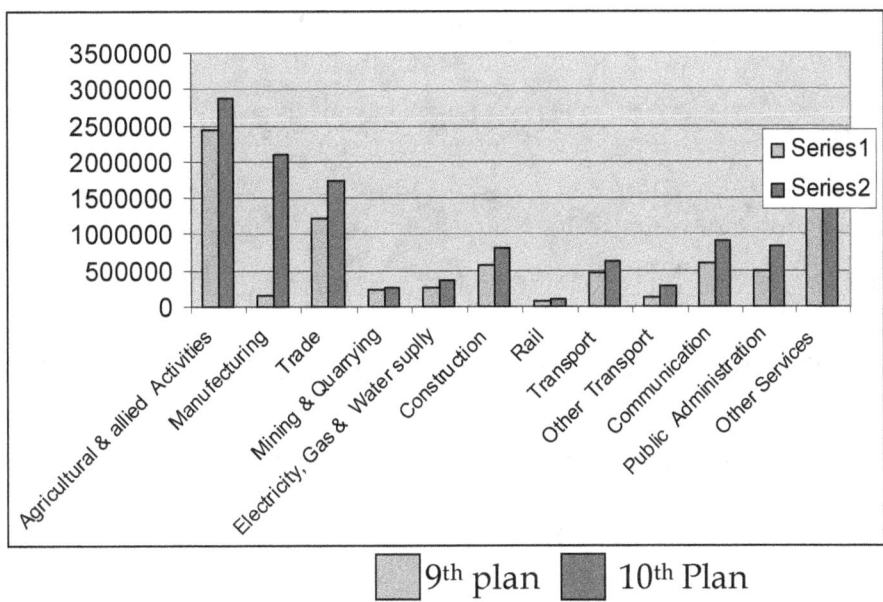

9th plan    10th Plan

- Increased mechanization

- Non-food crops

- Importance to co-operatives

- Enhancement of dairying, poultry

- Use of more irrigated land, pump sets

- Use of non-conventional energy sources and

- Increased farming knowledge about use of fertilizers, pesticides and farming.

- **Increase in income:** The Government of India has been allocating large funds year after year for the planned growth of rural economy and agriculture. Cultivators have taken up high yield cash crops and multi-cropping. This has reduced dependence on seasons. The disposal income with villagers is on the increase. Job opportunities in villages have increased due to various government schemes for rural employment. Minimum agriculture labour wages and procurement prices of cereals have also increased. All this has substantially been increasing the purchasing power of the common villager.

- **Improvement in infrastructure:** With efforts from state and local bodies, the road connections, transport and communication facilities in villages have improved. This has impact m increased market reach.

- **Increase in expectations:** Contact with urban population and faster communications lave increased the expectations of a general villager. The lifestyles are changing to modern and here are potential consumers in the villages. Consumerism is thus entering the villages in a big way.

With plus points as detailed above in village social-economic areas, the marketing of agricultural produce has the following challenges:

(i) Transport and distribution: All "weather" roads are lacking to nearly 30 percentages of the villages. In the rainy season, it is not possible to reach many of them. The agricultural product cannot move,

(ii) Communication: The low level of literacy is the main hurdle in village communication. In this area, telephones and mobile phones are helping to bridge a large extent the communication gap.

(iii) Scattered villages: There are 5.7 lakh villages. The movement of produce from villages to town and between villages poses challenges. The distances make the operations on many occasions uneconomical.

(iv) Warehousing facilities: The nature of commodities needs special warehousing and transport. Such warehouses are not available in adequate number. There is considerable wastage,

(v) Inadequate credit facilities: A villager producing agricultural goods face problems in getting funds at the right time due to procedural hassles. This makes the business cycle to come to a halt.

(vi) Segmentation: The requirements of agricultural products vary from place to place, income levels, tastes, seasons etc.

(vii) Nature of commodities: the perishable nature of commodities make the price

(viii) Middle men: the middle men take away the cake in terms of monetary benefit marketing the producer poor.

(ix) Low productivity: in developing countries, there is considerable disguised unemployment the traditional practices do not go. These make low productivity in the agricultural sector.

(x) Seller's market: the large population in underdeveloped countries makes more demand on the produce. It is a seller's market and whatever is produced is sold. In such a situation production of quantities gets importance

(xi) Low market intelligence: due to scarcity, the markets are production-oriented. The customer's wants and expectations have little place. The data is not available on customer and results in low industrialisation.

(xii) Non-monetised sectors in economy due to vicious circle of poverty are low. Considerable non-monetised transaction takes place within cultural and historical background. The produce is distributed partly for services.

**Differences in Marketing of Agricultural and Manufactured Goods.**

| Sl. No. | Agricultural Produce | Industrial Goods |
|---|---|---|
| 1. | **Grown by villager or produce by villager** | **Manufactured in industries.** The agricultural products are sometimes used in industry like cotton, jute, eggs in bakeries, tobacco, fruits and pickles are canned cereals are ground and packed. These become agro-industry item. |
| 2. | **Production characteristic** | |
| | **a.** Variation in quality – agricultural produce is natural and quality differs as per seeds, inputs tending etc. | Uniformity in quality as per requirement or set parameter |
| | **b.** Production is bulky | Production is of uniform size |
| | **c.** Small scale production as land holding in India | Large or medium scale |
| | **d.** Seasonal | Not seasonal, regular |
| | **e.** Depends on rains and climate | Not dependent on climate |
| 3. | **Product** | |

| | | | |
|---|---|---|---|
| | **a.** Perishable. Each has a short shelf life | Lasts longer |
| | **b.** Not uniform in size or quality | Uniformity din product size and quality |
| | **c.** Not slandardised product | The end products are slandardised |
| | **d.** Packing difficult | All the product are nicely packed, making it attractive |
| **4.** | **Market commodities** | |
| | **a.** Scattered all over India | Target costumers. |
| | **b.** Finance flows irregular or at best seasonal | Regular finance activities. This makes finance planning easy |
| | **c.** Problems in handling and transport | No such problems |
| | **d.** Problems of proper roads | No such problems |
| | **e.** Problems of Communication | No such Problems |
| | **f.** Problems of distribution | Specialised distribution agencies are in place |
| | **g.** Segmentation id difficult | The market segmentation exists |
| | **h.** Middlemen play an important role | Middlemen are not necessary |
| | **i.** Imperfect market, no written documents | Nearly perfect markets-all in written documentation |
| | **j.** Inelastic or uncharged demand | Demand pattern change |
| | **k.** Absence of organized qualified buying or selling | Organized buying and selling exists |

## Commodities in Agricultural Marketing

Items of Agricultural marketing or rural marketing-out items and many can be classified into seven groups:

(i)   Horticulture produce

(ii)   Food grain items

(iii) Oilseed produce

(iv) Fibre produce

(v) Beverages items

(vi) Cash items and

(vii) Animal produce.

The horticulture items in class (i) above classified as flowers, spices, vegetables and fruits.

**History of Agricultural Marketing**

The history of growth and development of agricultural marketing is evolutionary, rich and an interesting one. From the available data, a broad picture can give. The problems in marketing of agricultural produce existed for generation. Only the volumes, distances and complexities have changed. The study of the past developments helps in emphasizing that changes are

continually underway. New developments from many different sources have always marketing practices and organisations to adapt or reorient these practices.

Though agriculture was started by early man around 8000 B.C., we have evidences of good agriculture around 2,500 B.C. in Harappa and Mohcnjodaro civilization. Early in the development of Indian community, people realised that some were better adapted to certain kinds of activities than others. Thus, they specialised in their work. This is referred to in history as development. Varna and caste systems. This specialisation increased the output of agricultural produce. It also removed self sufficiency of the family unit. They began to produce more than the requirement the family consumption. This facilitated the exchange of surplus commodities. The marketing tasks were evolved and also middlemen who specialize in this work entered.

The problems faced by them were:

- Transportation at a reasonable time and cost
- Perishable nature and hence losses
- Volume and trade qualities were limited and
- Communication

Until the fourth quarter of the nineteenth century, the agricultural pattern was one of the small industries with transportation and communication local nature. Cotton dispatches to England from India presented earlier transportation, packing handling and marketing problems, Grading was also major issue.

During the first half of the twentieth century, large famines, droughts and other natural calamities brought the focus of transportation and distribution problems of agricultural commodities in far flung places in India. Many an occasion imports and airlifting of food grains became necessary.

After Independence, India gave due importance to agriculture. With the Green Revolution, India had registered the expansion of agricultural produce. This sudden and good development made available vast amount of food grains to feed its large population. In the turbulent two and half decades, the agricultural marketing system was put under great pressure to move this new productive capacity into the hands of the consumer.

The 1980s brought a new set of agricultural marketing developments and issues. The struggle as keep agricultural produce supplies and demands in balance at prices acceptable to both farmers and consumers led to government interventions by way of subsidies, taxes, procurement and controls. Being a big vote bank, fanners could at times, dictate their points.

The 1990s were marked by consumption preferences by the consumers. Multinational food points, processed foods, ready to cook, instant and ready-to-eat commodities changed the market demand. Fast food joints started dolling the cities. The large food companies entered the scene in a big way.

Changes in agricultural production and agricultural marketing continue at a rapid rate. New marketing challenges and developments are in the area of: biotechnology, trade growth, globalization of markets, organic and natural foods, instant foods, direct marketing, specialty
siche or branded agricultural products.

# Chapter 2
## Growth of Agriculture

"Indian agriculture is bouncing back. It is scripting its own success story, thanks to rising private investment, which will lead to a faster growth. Faster growth in agriculture tomorrow will happen because of rising private investment in agriculture today,"

However, cautions that it is unrealistic to expect a repeat of last year's double-digit growth in agriculture, despite the forecast of a normal monsoon. Indian agriculture will grow faster than before.

Agribusiness companies are developing new models to reach out to farmers and consumers, providing new technologies, investing more in modern supply chains and in organized food retailing that sells more and more processed food.

The surge in private investment is due to increased demand for food and other agricultural commodities. With the income level rising, demand for milk, meat or fish, fruits and vegetables is also increasing. With more urbanisation, Indian families also consume more processed foods, more ready-to-eat foods, etc; India is becoming a medium-sized agricultural exporter, selling tea, fish, spices and now rice and wheat to foreign countries.

Smart businesses have realized that it is a growing opportunity to be present in any part of the agricultural value chain, which has led to more investment not only by big companies but even by first-generation entrepreneurs.

Improved rural infrastructure is also playing a key role behind the agri sector's comeback trail. With better rural infrastructure, is comparatively easier and cost-effective to bring farm produce to the market. Better rural roads, more godowns and cold storages, improving rural electricity supply, will all result in faster growth in agriculture.

Indian farmers are learning to take on the challenge of producing better quality produce at internationally competitive prices. They are willing to use new technologies, and become organized.

However, points out that Indian agriculture still suffer from:

- Poor productivity.

- Falling water levels.

- Expensive credit.

- A distorted market.

- Many intermediaries who increase cost but do not add much value.

- Laws that stifle private investment.

- Controlled prices.

- Poor infrastructure.

- Produce that does not meet international standards.

- Inappropriate research.

- Tax evasion by unorganized sector leading to the lack of a level playing field.

All these hamper the farmers and the Industry. In addition, agriculture is a state subject, and most states have little funds to invest in agriculture development. If these problems are removed, India can become the 'food factory of the world.'

Agricultural reforms and increased private investment must, benefit farmers, especially small farmers. Our opinion that farmers would benefit by greater corporate investment in agriculture, especially in three areas: getting competitive sources of finance; getting competitive markets to sell to; and getting competitive suppliers of knowledge.

According to CII, (The Confederation of Indian Industry) agriculture in 2004 is like industry was in 1991. The private sector was awaiting policy reforms that would allow it to make much larger investments in this sector.

CII's five main agri-reform agenda includes:

- Give States an incentive to amend the APMC act and abolish *mandi* taxes. This would allow competitive markets to develop; farmers and processors will both gain.

- Support the organised private sector in increasing its spending on extension and technology transfer. This would give farmers the knowledge of what to grow, and how to grow so that stringent quality norms are met.

- Implement the Unified Food Law, and back it up with lowering the total tax burden on processed foods so that the sector picks up, and consequently demand for farm produce rises.

- Target foreign buyers of high-value ethnic Indian foods, as opposed to commodity exports-starting with the large NRI population of 20 million, which can be a huge market.

Create a viable model of public-private partnership that allows private investors to invest in agriculture infrastructure in partnership with banks and financial institutions.

# GROWTH OF AGRICULTURAL MARKETING

**(i) Area:** India is a vast country and it is commonly believed that it has unlimited, area for agriculture purpose. This is not true. Out of the total geographical area, net area has sown accounts for 46.6 per cent, out of which irrigated land is around 23 per cent. The land use classification is detailed in Fig.8.5 below.

From this figure it may be seen that land has been broadly divided; (a) Forests - 22.2 percentage, (b) not available for cultivation - 13.4 percentage, (c) Other uncultivated land - 10.0 percentage, (d) Fallow lands - 23.4 percentage, (e) Net area sown is 46.6 percentage, out of which 23.2 percentage) is gross irrigated land. There is growth in the net sown area and net irrigated land since the last five decades.

**(ii) Marketing efforts:** The marketing of agricultural produce has fuelled growth since independence. 'Market first, their produce the product' has been the corner stone. Marketing influences, volume, variety and price of agricultural supplies.

In the past, a fanner produced whatever traditionally he produced. He used to call "Gift of Mother Earth". It was presumed that consumers will buy and use whatever produced. Today's farmer's decisions are made based on marketer's and consumer's decisions. The producer now produces what the consumer needs. Markets want value. There is close inter-relationship between the marketer and agricultural producer. In the process, the doctrine of consumer sovereinity is honored, marketing activities have spead to all corners of India and overseas.

**(iii)Large growth:** Since independence, Indian agricultural marketing and production has witnessed a four fold growth. This is highest in the Indian agriculture history.

### Land use Classification -1993-94

|  |  |  | Million Hectares |
| --- | --- | --- | --- |
| Sl. No. | Items | 1993-94 | percentage to reporting Area |
|  |  |  |  |

| 1. | Geographical area | 328.73 | |
|---|---|---|---|
| 2. | Reporting area for land utilization Statistics | 305.01 | |
| | (i) Forest | 67.99 | 22.2 |
| | (ii) Not available for cultivation (A+B) | 40.88 | 13.4 |
| | (A) Area under non-agricultural uses | 21.22 | 7.0 |
| | (B) Barren and unculturable land | 19.66 | 6.4 |
| | (iii) Other uncultivated land excluding fallow (A+B+C) | 30.51 | 10.0 |
| | (A) Permanent pastures and other grazing lands | 11.80 | 3.9 |
| | (B) Land under miscellaneous tree crops | 3.70 | 1.2 |
| | (C) Culturable waste | 15.01 | 4.9 |
| | (iv) Fallow lands (A+B) | 23.40 | 7.7 |
| | (A) Fallow land other than current follows | 9.59 | 3.2 |
| | (B) Current follows | 13.80 | 4.5 |
| | (v) Net area sown | 142.24 | 46.6 |
| 3. | Gross cropped area | 185.48 | 60.8 |
| 4. | Area sown more than once | 42.24 | 14.2 |
| 5. | Net area irrigated | 47.43 | 15.5 |
| 6. | Gross area irrigated | 70.64 | 23.2 |

(Source: NIRD Rural Development Statistics, 1998, Page 75)

The productions of major crops are detailed in figure. From the figure, it may be noted that food grains have grown four in five decades and milk production has gone up five fold Sugarcane and cotton have increased to five fold.

**Production of Major Crops and Allied Ili'ins (1950-51 to 1996-97)**

| Crops | 1950-51 | 1970-71 | 1980-81 | 1990-91 | 1996-97 | 2002-03 |
|---|---|---|---|---|---|---|
| | | | | | | (Million Tone) |
| Food grains | 50.82 | 103.42 | 129.59 | 179.39 | 199.32 | 183.20 |
| Rice | 20.58 | 42.22 | 53.63 | 74.29 | 81.31 | 77.70 |
| Wheat | 6.46 | 23.83 | 36.31 | 55.14 | 69.27 | 68.90 |
| C.Cereals | 15.38 | 30.55 | 29.02 | 32.70 | 34.28 | 75.10 |
| Pluses | 8.41 | 11.82 | 10.63 | 14.26 | 14.46 | 11.50 |
| Sugarcane | 57.05 | 126.37 | 154.25 | 241.05 | 277.25 | 285.40 |
| Cotton (in bales) | 3.04 | 4.76 | 7.01 | 9.84 | 14.25 | 8.90 |
| Nine Oilseeds | 5.16 | 9.63 | 9.37 | 18.61 | 24.96 | 15.40 |
| Milk | 17.00 | 21.20 | 31.60 | 53.90 | 68.60 | 84.60 |
| Fish | .80 | 1.80 | 2.40 | 3.80 | 5.35 | 6.00 |

(Source: Ninth five year Plan,1997-2002, Vol.II. Page.435, Ministry of Agricultural)

**(iv)Science and Technology:** Since the late sixties, there is surge of production due to technolgoy and science inputs. The Green Revolution in India during the period helped the matter. This gave better yields and tended to be labour saving. The agricultural productivity increased to a large extent during the period. Fig. 8.7 on the next page shows the productivity of agriculture trends since 1650 AD. From the graph it may be seen that since 1950, there is a growth of fifty per cent. It is science and not land that has made this possible.

**(v) Improvement in Inputs:** Large improvements have taken place in recent years in terms of better seeds, livestock nutrition, fertilisers, pesticides and variety of other inputs. Science has shown that two plants can be grown where one was possible earlier. The plants are healthy and give more yield. The produce has better shelf life. Longer storages helps in reducing spoilage or wastages and give better returns. There is pressure to move agricultural produce and this added production into consumption. The volume of agricultural produce has increased but also the increasing portion of this has moved into commercial and global marketing channels.

Specilisation in agri-produce are changing ways how to produce and market the products.

**(vi) Government Policies:** During the post-independence period, the agricultural growth rate works out to about 2-7 per cent per annum. As per the Ninth Five Year Plan (1997-2002) Report Vol II,Pg.434, this figure is much higher than the negligible growth rate of 0.3 per cent per annum in the first half of the twentieth century. India has attained self sufficiency in food grains at existing consumption levels and with some surplus for export purpose. Good change is due to increasing consumption levels and marketing efforts in addition to science and technology inputs. The Government has given top priority to agriculture in the nine five year plans. In the proposed Tenth five year plan also, emphasis has been given to agriculture. Government has given direct and indirect encouragement to agriculture in giving tax concessions, subsidy procurement pricing, building infrastructure and controlling prices of inputs like fertilisers. percentages of agriculture expenditure in total planned outlays are higher. In 50s, the percentage used to be 32 whereas it has come to 11 per cent in the Ninth plan period. Fig. 8.8 gives details of total outlays and expenditure on agriculture in the Ninth five year plan periods. There are considerable wastages inspite of growth in agriculture due to mismatch in supply chain and storage facilities.

**(vii)Change of Mindset:** Since the Green Revolution of late sixties, there is a change of mindset of the Indian farmer. He has oriented himself to the market. Export is one area he is looking with keen interest. With the change of mindset, the old methods of working are changing fast. The old trends and new trends in the agri-business are detailed in Figure.

Use of computers and programmes thereon are helping farmers in Government bodies are showing the way as to how to access information on markets. Earlier new technologies tended to be labour saving, in recent decades, it is now yield enhancing.

The below figure shows a software package developed by Tata Consultancy Service "Kishan Net" as

Government is an innovative arrangement made by Government of Andhra Pradesh for farmers to sell agricultural produce directly to consumers. Farmers today have many alternatives. With reliable information on hand, the farmer can choose optional alternate courses.

## Agricultural Development during Five Year Plans

| Outlay expenditure | First Plan 1951-56 | Second Plan 1965-61 | Third Plan 1961-66 | Annual Plan 1966-69 | Fourth Plan 1969-74 | Fifth Plan 1974-78 | Sixth Plan 1980-85 | Seven Plan 1985-90 | Eight Plan 1992-97 | Ninth Plan 1997-2002 |
|---|---|---|---|---|---|---|---|---|---|---|
| Total public Outlay | 2,378 | 4,800 | 8,577 | 6,665 | 15,902 | 39,303 | 9,500 | 1,80,000 | 4,34,100 | 8,59,200 |
| Agriculture and community | 360 | 565 | 1,089 | 1,051 | 2,385 | - | 5,695 | 10,524 | 22,467 | 42,462 |
| Development irrigation and food control | 400 | 485 | 664 | 445 | 1,087 | - | 12,160 | 16,979 | 32,525 | 55,420 |
| Total expenditure on Agriculture | 760 | 1,023 | 1,753 | 1,496 | 3,472 | 8,253 | 17,855 | 27,503 | 54,992 | 97,882 |
| percentages of Agriculture Expenditure in Total public outlay | 32 | 21 | 20 | 22 | 22 | 21 | 18 | 15 | 12 | 11 |

Note: 1. Expenditure on every for farm operation is not included in the total expenditure on agriculture, since it is not available

2. Plan-wise absolute figure of expenditure are not comparable due to fall in the value of money. Comparison of the percentages is free from this limitation.

(Source: (i) Five Year Plan Reports, (ii) NIED Rural Development Statistics, 1998)

## Agriculture Sector and GDP Growth

The country is on development way (path). According to expert conclusion due to industry and services sector in India, GDP growth rate will be in double digit in nearest future and various sector in India, which have variety of development opportunity are there, in which retailing and agriculture sector are first, because of 70 percentage of population in India is depends on agriculture. And where majority part of population of country depends on agriculture. Its not possible to development as a whole without join this sector with main source. In short, if India wants to development as a whole and double its GDP growth than agriculture sector can't be avoid.

According to expert view development of agriculture sector can be possible by two way. The opportunity for production of agriculture and employment opportunity will increase with development of industry and urbanization for that care should be taken that how industry development reach to the rural area. The link should be maintain between urban and rural economy. The per capital income will be increase with the growth of industry but rural area it's still background. The demand for the vegetable, fruits and dairy products will be increase the development of industry, in urban area. Thus indirectly industry development will make possible development for rural area. Private companies and agencies should co-operate to villages for providing them development advantages. Working system should be maintain the marketing of dairy and agriculture products than only advantages of development reach to village people and standard of living will be increase and for that the goods should be directly purchased from farmers for achieving produce demand by making strong retailing chain. Now a day's miss management is found in this two condition. So farmers can't get the enough advantage so join the agricultural sector with main sources for double GDP growth

(Source: Gujarat Samachar, 13th December 2006, Wednesday, Page 4)

## TRADINATIONAL RURAL SYSTEM

The traditional rural system was to treat agricultural production for sustenance and not for growth and prosperity. Most of the people treated, ups and downs in the production of crops as the grace of the God or effects of devils. Total dependence on rains, natural manure, selecting an auspicious day and time for seeding and cutting the crops were the hallmark of traditional system of Indian Agriculturists.

From the marketing point of few, there was no serious effort for sending materials to other states and district places. Export of goods was not known. Hence the selling of excess produce was mainly in towns around the village. At the district level, it was a big market area in olden days. Use of chemical fertilisers, HYV seeds and productivity are recent trends and hence the present situation and pre-independence situation of agricultural production and marketing are not comparable.

Another drawback of the old system was transport, movement (of people) and communication, this was especially more relevant to short life products/goods like fruits, vegetables, flowers, fish and dairy products. Unless these are transported very fast, the value of the products gets

reduced. Hence, the rural producer was unable to get a good price for short life products.

The 'Cash Crops' idea was not known. People were content to grow grains which are required for physiological needs. Important crops were wheat, jowar, rice, pulses and sugarcane. Fruits and vegetables were grown without proper plan and use of manures. Naturally the farmer's produce was in the buyer's market.

## GOVERNMENT INTERVENTION IN AGRO-MARKETING

During the British rule, marketing conditions varied from province to province and in respect of different products. The first government intervention started in 1928 when the Vice-Roy formed Royal Commission on Agriculture' to recommend improvement measures.

The Committee fell, that information on agriculture markets is inadequate and suggested control on free trade of agricultural commodities in all stages from production to consumption. Since in some provinces like Madras, CP and Berar the marketing was efficient and in other states it was not satisfactory. Hence, the Commission suggested to remove local autonomy to standardise wrights, measures and taxes for all provinces. This was to be adopted in some way as in England at that time. In 1930, provincial legislations to regulate markets were drafted and in 1933, Madras Commercial Crops Markets Act was formulated.

There was a practice of brokers representing both buyers and sellers and taking commission from both. The Government imposed prohibition of such dual representation. The regulated markets were functioning for the wholesale trade of selected commodities.

## Regulation of Agricultural Marketing

One of the important topics of DMI (Directorate of Marketing and Inspection) was to organise Agricultural Marketing Regulations in India. For this, it was essential to formulate marketing legislations for imposing control standards for agricultural products.

In the post-independence era, agriculture was given higher priority in economic growth, It was essential to take refamative steps in the interest of producers as well as consumers. Some of the important legislations passed towards the reformations are as follows:

- Forword Contracts (Regulation) Act 1951.
- The Emblems and Names (Prevention of Improper Use) Act, 1950.
- The Drugs Control Act, 1950.
- The Indian Standard Institution (Certification of Money) Act 1952 (Now it is called Bureau of Indian Standards).
- The Prevention of Food Adulteration Act, 1954.
- The Essential Commodities Act, 1955 and

- The Standards of Weights and Measures Act, 1976.

Above legislations have undergone changes and amendments from time to time, keeping in view the changes and, needs of emerging situations. Legislations are carried out to help the consumers.

# Chapter 3
## About Unjha Market Yard

### 1. Establishment:-

The Agricultural Market Committee, Unjha is established on Dt.:- 23-10-'54 (1954-55) under the Bombay Agricultural Produce Act.-1939 (Bombay XXII) for the better regulation of purchase and sale of Agricultural Commodities in Market area.

There are 26 villages of Unjha Taluka in the market area of this Committee and Unjha is declared as principal Market Yard in the Market area Arrivals of Agricultural Commodities in Unjha Market Yard is from 300K.M. redius i.e. Mehsana Dist., Sabarkantha Dist., Banaskantha Dist., Saurath, Kutch, and Rajasthan in the Market area to extend sale and purchase facilities.

"27" Agricultural Commodities Viz. Jeera (Cumin), Variali (Fennel Seeds), Isabgul, Sarsav, Raido (Mustard), Castor Seeds, Till, Groundnuts, Asalio, Rajgaro, Fenugreek, Moong, Math, Udad, Gram, Tur, Val, Chola,

Guwar, Wheat, Bajari, Juvar, Chino, Kalingada-Bij, Cotton, Coriander Seeds, Vegetable & Fruits, Suwa (Dill Seeds), Ajmo (Ajwain Seeds), in the Market area.

## 2. Object:-

The object of Market Act. Is to regulate the Market for protecting Agriculturist sellers by cash and kind to established modern Market Yard with required facilities for producers and traders.

## 3. Constitution of Market Committee:-

The Market Committee is constituted of 17 members, i.e. 8 (Eight) Agriculturalist, 2 (Two) Member from Co.Op.Sale Society, 4 (Four), Traders, 1 (One) Local Authority and 2 (Two) government nominees. These 17 Members elect one of them as Chairman and a Vice-Chairman and there after it comes through election at every four years.

The Committee appoints Secretary and necessary staff under the approval of the director of Agricultural

Marketing & Rural finance, Gujarat State, Gandhinagar. Who is the executive authority of the act.

## 4. Importance of Unjha Market:-

Unjha Market Yard is one of the biggest regulated Market and it a well known commercial centre throughout India for its trade Jeera (Cumin), Variali (Fennel Seeds), Isabgul and Raido (Mustard Seeds) crop of Jeera, Variali and Isabgol is only possible in North Gujarat is superior in quality and hence there is great demand from all over India and foreign Countries also.

Unjha is natural assembling and exporting centre for Agricultural Commodities of North Gujarat. There are 800 big business firms in this town which export Jeera, Variali, Oil Seeds, Pulses and Isabgul to nearly 1500 centre of India & foreign countries every year.

This Market is also important for cursing and grinding of Oilseeds, Pulses, Isabgul, Coriander seeds and Kalingada-bil etc. There are 6 Oil mills, 5 Pulses mills, 4 Sat Issabgul factories, 27 cleaning factories for Jeera, Variali and other spices, 6 Kalingada-baji factories & 5 Coriander seeds factories in Unjha.

Thus Unjha is natural assembling and exporting centre of Agricultural Commodities.

## 5. Facilities of the Market:-

Unjha Market is situated on the main line of the Western Railway Ahmedabad-Delhi State high-way is also passing through the outskirts of this town. There is a Post Office, Telegraph and Telephone services, 17 Banks and Sub treasury, State warehouse. Thus Unjha Market has all the modern facilities of transports, Communication, Banking and storages etc. for the trade.

## 6. Progress in the Regulation of the Market:-

Before the application of the Act. Unjha Market was unregulated and it was running on own accord of traders. Facilities of open auction (sale) standard weightment, cash payment protection from malpractice's and amenities were not provided to agrits sellers by way.

After the application of the Act. The Market Committee has introduce the following main features of regulation.

**Method of Sale:-**

The Agricultural Commodities brought for the sale in the Market Yard are arranged in open heaps in the plots allotted to general commission agent and heaps are sold through open auction conducted by the paid auctioneers of the Committee. The detail of sale is noted by auction clerks on the same times. This detail is useful for solution disputes.

**Sieving and Delivery:-**

After auction all the produce is sieved for minimizing adulteration and for improving Agricultural Commodities. According to the serial order of the delivery of the produce is taken in the Market Yard on the place of auction by standard weights and standardized on the spot i.e. real weight is given.

**Cash Payment:-**

After talking delivery of the produce a cash memo is prepared by the general commission agent or purchaser and one of memo is given to the seller with cash payment another to Market Committee and copy is kept for his own record. Thus cash payment is introduce in all the work of sales delivery & payment is finished on the same say of arrivals & the commission agent prepares a sales slip in triplicate, one copy given to purchaser, one given to Market Committee with Market fees and one for his own record and recover the value of sale from the purchaser next day with Market fee.

## 7. Dissemination of Price:-

Daily price and arrivals of the Market is published on notice board and broadcasted on Radio amplifier, Baroda Centre.

## 8. Site of Unjha Market Yard and Sub-Yard:-

The present site of Unjha Market Yard is between Unjha town and railway station with an area of acres 36.37G. having all necessary facilities. Due to heavy arrivals of regulated Commodities at Unjha Market Yard., Market Committee. Unjha has purchase acres 45.15 GF. of land at Unava Village (5kms. Away from Unjha on Highway) for sub-Market Yard and has prepared a layout plan with all necessary modern facilities 416 office-cum-Godowns estimated at a cost Rs. 5 Corers. 33 vegetables shop, 2 Rural godown facility in sub yars Unava.

As per Government of Gujarat Agricultural co-operation and Gram Development section, Gandhinasgar vide their order serial No. G.H.K.H.-9/ 97/ APMC/1197/ 1076/ G-26 Dated 31-01-'97, the APMC, Unjha and APMC, Unava has been separated and given it's own identity.

# Chapter 4
## Research Methodology

**Objectives:-**

- To study the marketing activities established by Unjha Market Yard.

- To study the reason of selecting Unjha Market Yard by Farmers.

- To study the problems faced by the farmers and traders  regarding their products.

- To analyze the farmers and traders satisfaction about the marketing services provided by Unjha Market Yard.

**Questionnaire:-**

A separate questionnaire was prepared for consumer to obtain the necessary feed back and data. Farmers and traders in Unjha Market Yard were interviewed and requested to answer the questionnaire containing 15 questions. All these were contacted personally to avoid any misunderstanding, misinterpretation and possible confusion. In this way personal interview method adopted.

**Research Methodology:-**

**Research design: - Descriptive type of Research**

This study is based on descriptive research, which is very regal design of study and the procedure to be used, must be carefully planned. The first study is to diversify objective, methods of data collection and selection of sample analysis are to be planned.

In this study there is a preplanning of study measures we had first formulated objectives and then follow the entire procedure of descriptive type of research.

**Sources of Data:-**

In order to achieve the objective of the present study, There are two types of data collection method.

**(A) Primary Data    (B) Secondary Data**

**(A) Primary Data:-**

Primary Data are collected directly by the researcher for the first time to the best of the knowledge and belief of the researcher, Asset of interviewers with    **1). Farmers. 2). Traders.**

**(B)  Secondary Data:-**

Secondary Data are collected complied and publish by Unjha Market Yard and others and a researcher problem.

Libraries, Literature, Periodicals, Journals, Annual Reports and other relevant records maintained by Market Committee.

**Data Collection Method:-**

In this study, I used a personal survey method which is the face to face questioning and answering to Farmers and Traders.

**Field Work:-**

The present study was carried out in Unjha Market Yard at Mehsana District of Gujarat State. Unjha is the one of the biggest Market Yard for cumin, fennel and psyllium (Isabgul) in INDIA.

**Sampling Plan:-**

**Sample Unit: -**

The sampling unit in appropriate size would be down from various respondents.

**Sample Size:-**

A sample of fifty (50) Farmers and Fifteen (15) Traders will be taken from the Unjha Market Yard.

**Sampling Method:-**

The data will collect from the respondents with the help of specially designed schedules. The data will analyze by expressing the data in simple percentage terms.

## Limitation of the Study:-

As very coin has two side, the research study also have two side. There are certain limitations, which deceives the object of the study.

### 1  Area:-

The research study has been conducted only at Unjha Market Yard.

### 2.  Time:-

The research was done in very limited time of four months.

### 3.  Sample Size:-

The sample size prefixed for the research study was of 50 Farmers and 15 Traders.

# Chapter 5
## RESULTS

## 1. Classification of Facilities provided to farmers by Unjha Market Yard.

| Sr. No. | Facilities | Respondents | Percentage of Respondents |
|---------|------------|-------------|---------------------------|
| 1. | High Price | 31 | 62 |
| 2. | Proper Weight Facilities | 50 | 100 |
| 3. | Transportation Facilities | 50 | 100 |
| 4. | Cash Payment Facilities | 48 | 96 |
| 5. | Provide update price of goods | 11 | 22 |

## 2. Commodity wise earning of Farmers:

| Sr. No. | Commodity | Respondents | Percentage of Respondents |
|---------|-----------|-------------|---------------------------|
| 1. | Cumin | 47 | 94 |
| 2. | Fennel | 12 | 24 |
| 3. | Isabgul | 12 | 24 |
| 4. | Any Other | 9 | 18 |

## 3. Losses suffered by Farmers due to Holiday:-

| Sr. No. | Losses | Respondents | Percentage of Respondents |
|---|---|---|---|
| 1. | Weight | 10 | 20 |
| 2. | Price | 22 | 44 |
| 3. | Quality | 5 | 10 |
| 4. | Any Other | 0 | 0 |

## 4. Information provides by Unjha Market Yard to Farmers:

| Sr. No. | Information | Respondents | Percentage of Respondents |
|---|---|---|---|
| 1. | Fertilizers | 47 | 94 |
| 2. | Machinery | 10 | 20 |
| 3. | Pesticides | 44 | 88 |
| 4. | Seeds | 15 | 30 |

## 5. Data publication of UNJHA MARKET YARD

| Sr. No. | Publication | Respondents | percentage of Respondents |
|---|---|---|---|
| 1. | News Paper | 48 | 96 |
| 2. | Magazine | 8 | 16 |
| 3. | Annual Reports | 44 | 88 |
| 4. | Price List | 40 | 80 |

## 6. Social Responsibility perform by UNJHA MARKET YARD

| Sr. No. | Social Responsibility | Respondents | percentage of Respondents |
|---|---|---|---|
| 1. | Education | 49 | 98 |
| 2. | Sport | 15 | 30 |
| 3. | Medicine | 46 | 92 |
| 4. | Rural & Urban Development | 43 | 86 |

## 7. Classification of bad experience of farmers with Unjha Market Yard.

| Sr. No. | Bad Experience | Respondents | percentage of Respondents |
|---|---|---|---|
| 1. | Price | 15 | 30 |
| 2. | Weight | 7 | 14 |
| 3. | Payment | 0 | 0 |
| 4. | Infrastructure Facility | 2 | 4 |

## 8. Educational Qualification Wise Classification of Farmers.

| Sr. No. | Education Qualification | Respondents | percentage of Respondents |
|---|---|---|---|
| 1. | Below S.S.C. | 8 | 16 |
| 2. | S.S.C. | 27 | 54 |
| 3. | H.S.C. | 15 | 30 |
| 4. | Graduate | 0 | 0 |
| 5. | Post Graduate | 0 | 0 |

- **Data analysis interpretation ( Traders-20)**

## 1. Classification Of Facilities Provided By Unjha Market Yard To Traders.

| Sr. No. | Facilities | Respondents | percentage of Respondents |
|---|---|---|---|
| 1. | Credit facility | 7 | 35 |
| 2. | Price information | 20 | 100 |
| 3. | Co-ordination | 10 | 50 |
| 4. | Prevent of fire facility | 20 | 100 |
| 5. | Infrastructure facility | 20 | 100 |
| 6. | Exporting facility | 19 | 95 |
| 7. | Storage facility | 13 | 65 |

## 2. Calling trading meeting by Unjha Market Yard.

| Sr. No. | Time Duration | Respondents | percentage of Respondents |
|---|---|---|---|
| 1. | Weekly | 0 | 0 |
| 2. | 15 Days | 1 | 5 |
| 3. | Monthly | 16 | 80 |
| 4. | Six Months | 4 | 20 |
| 5. | Yearly | 0 | 0 |

## 3. Classification of Bad experiences of Traders with Unjha Market Yard

| Sr. No. | Bad Experiences | Respondents | percentage of Respondents |
|---------|-----------------|-------------|---------------------------|
| 1. | High Price | 1 | 5 |
| 2. | Quality | 4 | 20 |
| 3. | Any Other | 0 | 0 |

## 4. Commodity wise earning of Traders:

| Sr. No. | Commodities | Respondents | percentage of Respondents |
|---------|-------------|-------------|---------------------------|
| 1. | Cumin | 20 | 100 |
| 2. | Fennel | 3 | 15 |
| 3. | Isabgul | 1 | 5 |
| 4. | Any Other | 4 | 20 |

## 5. Losses suffered by Traders during Holiday

| Sr. No. | Losses | Respondents | percentage of Respondents |
|---------|--------|-------------|---------------------------|
| 1. | Weight | 0 | 0 |
| 2. | Price | 0 | 0 |
| 3. | Quality | 1 | 5 |

## 6. Education Qualification wise Classification of Traders.

| Sr. No. | Education Qualification | Respondents | Percentage of respondents |
|---|---|---|---|
| 1. | Below S.S.C. | 1 | 5 |
| 2. | S.S.C. | 4 | 20 |
| 3. | H.S.C. | 9 | 45 |
| 4 | Graduate | 6 | 30 |
| 5. | Post Graduate | 0 | 0 |

# Chapter 6
## Findings and Suggestions:-
### Findings:-

- There are so many facilities provided by Unjha Market Yard to farmers but most of important facilities are proper weight facilities, transportation facility and cash payment facility provided and less important facility is provide up-date price of goods.

- 94 percentage farmers earn by cumin and less earn by other commodities.

- Due to holiday 44 percentage farmers suffered by price loss.

- Most of the farmers are getting fertilizers and pestisides information by Unjha Market Yard

- Unjha Market Yard mostly published there data in newspapers, annual reports and price list and sometime published in any magazines.

- 98 percentage farmers attend meeting organized by Unjha Market Yard in this meeting most of the suggestion excepted by Unjha Market Yard.

- Most of the responsibilities are performed by Unjha Market Yard i.e. education, medicine, urban and rural development but perform less in sports responsibility.

- Most of the farmer's education qualification is S.S.C. and H.S.C.

- There are so many facilities provided by Unjha Market Yard to traders but main facilities are price information facility, prevent of fire facility, infrastructure facility and exporting facility provided and less facility provided are credit facility by Unjha Market Yard.

- 100 percentage traders attend meeting organized by Unjha Market Yard. Unjha Market Yard is calling trading meeting mostly monthly suggestions are also excepted by Unjha Market Yard.

- 20 percentage traders suffered by bad experience for quality in Unjha Market Yard.

- 100 percentage traders earn profit by cumin and less by Isabgul.

- During holiday traders suffered by quality loss.

- Most of the trader's education qualification is H.S.C. and graduate.

**Suggestions:-**

- The price updation of goods should be provided for farmers by published latest price list in magazines and any other publication and also maintain good relation with farmers.

- During holiday open subsidiary market for farmers and traders should be provide to avoid the price and quality loss suffered by farmers and trader.

- Provide the awareness of new agricultural machinery, technology and seeds to farmers.

- The sports responsibility for nearest villagers should be perform.

- Payment should be provided by cash credit or short term loan to the traders.

- The storages and price updation of commodities should be provided for reduce the quality loss.

- Price of important commodities should be written on the front page of newspapers, Notice board of the Market Yard offices and main city.

# References

- R.V. Badi and N.V.Badi "Rural Marketing" published by Himalaya Publishing house, Mumbai, First edition-2004.

- Annual reports of UNJHA MARKET YARD 2000-01 to 2005-06.

- Dr. M. L. Verma " International trade" Published by Vikash Publishing Pvt. Ltd., Reprint, 1996.

- Jain Sharad Chandra " Principles and Practics of agriculture marketing and prices".

- C.R. Kothari " Research Methodology" Methods and Techniques Published by Willey Eastern Limited, New Delhi.

- David J. Luck " Marketing Research" Published Prentice hall of India Pvt. Ltd., Seventh edition, New Delhi.

- Chairman. The Agricultural produce Market committee Unjha "Annual Report 2000-01 to 2005-06"

- V.S. Ramaswamy and S. Namakumari "Marketing Management" Planning, Implementation and control published by Mcmillan India Ltd, New Delhi.

- N.L. Agrawal and Narendra Singh "Agricultural Marketing" a case study of cumin seed marketing in Rajasthan.

- Newspapers- Gujarat Samachar, Sandesh, Times of India.

- www.Indiainbusiness.nic.in